Revelations For Resilience

WHISPERS FROM THE DIVINE FOR SOUL CARE

ANDREYAH MARIA HERNANDEZ BLACK

Revelations for Resilience

WHISPERS FROM THE DIVINE FOR SOUL CARE

ANDREYAH MARIA HERNANDEZ BLACK

"Be strong and of a good courage, fear not, nor be afraid of them: for the LORD thy God, he *it is* that doth go with thee; he will not fail thee, nor forsake thee."

~ Deuteronomy 31:6 (KJV)

REVELATIONS FOR RESILIENCE
Whispers from the Divine for Soul Care

Copyright © 2025
by
AndreYah Maria Hernandez Black

All rights reserved. No part of this book may be reproduced, stored in a retrieval system, or transmitted in any form or by any means—electronic, mechanical, photocopying, recording, or otherwise—without prior written permission from the publisher, except for brief quotations in reviews or critical articles.

Photographs Contributors:

AndreYAH M H Black (AMH Black), Almetra Murdock, Alexandre Neishtadt, and professional Russian photographer, Pavel Antonov. All photos in this book are copyrighted and may not be used without the permission of the Author

Book Cover Illustration, Angel:

Artist: Breten Bryden, www.BrydenArt.com
©All Rights Reserved

Angel:

Artist: Hilda Rank, courtesy of her daughter Anna Rank, www.AnnaRank.com
©All Rights Reserved

Cover & Inside Book Design

Henry Lucky Kalule,
Precision Media Limited
info.precisionmedia@gmail.com, Kampala Uganda-East Africa

ISBN: 979-8-218-87685-2 (Hardcover)

Published by

Bridgeport, Connecticut

DEDICATION

TO MY PARENTS OF LATE

My mother, the late Reverend Ramona Theon Black, was a compassionate and dedicated teacher for 25 years. She was my most cherished angel and confidante who exemplified dignity and integrity, always authentic and unwavering in her values; often viewed as old-fashioned. She devoted herself to raising her four daughters, including me, with a strict yet loving upbringing. Daily, she offered me seasoned, spiritual and prophetic guidance. Her wisdom instilled an old-fashioned Southern protocol: to attend church, cultivate a relationship with God, strive for higher education, take the higher road, and become one's best in one's vocation.

Through her exemplary lifestyle, my dear mother encouraged me to become the woman of integrity that I am today. One of her memorable sayings, shared before she transitioned to glory, was, *"It does not matter where you begin; what truly counts is how you finish."* She and my father instilled many spiritual lessons during my youth, which, to this day, I will never forget. My parents, particularly my mother, imparted numerous spiritual lessons during my upbringing that I still cherish today. Below, is one of the many scriptures she instilled in me as a child.

"I can do all things through Christ which strengtheneth me." *Philippians 4:13, KJV*

My father, the late Gilbert Hernandez Black, was my best friend and also one of the kindest and wisest fathers I could have ever asked for. His presence and support during my season of healing provided what I needed most. As far back as I can remember, my Dad gave me the strength and bravery to accomplish anything. In that season, he said, "Turn the page and start a new chapter." Honestly, this was not an easy thing to do; it took a while, yet I'm alive today to say, I made great progress.

ACKNOWLEDGMENTS

My appreciation is for the people in my life who supported me with all of their hearts during my tumultuous period spanning 2016 - 2018. Throughout my season, the names of the people below have proven to be a constant source of encouragement for me and deserve credit.

In a world that constantly demands more, hyper-independence forces single women to wear the exhausting armor of a superwoman, carrying everything while running on empty.

We must embrace community and avoid isolation to fully experience the wholeness and peace that God intended for our lives.

Thank you to my father of late, "Daddy"; Almetra; Uncle Jay; Aunt Bernadine; Aunt Joyce; Anita; Carmelita; Reverend Dr. Georgianna; and the faithful women of God—Val, Evelyn, and Sylvia—who called me nearly every day to pray, encourage, and bear my burdens.

ENDORSEMENTS

"AndreYAH's writings bring the reader to the very throne room of the Almighty. Read them slowly and absorb their wisdom. This is a book to treasure, to keep, and to give to others in your life who need a fresh touch from heaven."

Mrs. Anita Baird, Retired Principal

★★★

"In this autobiographical book, AndreYAH writes about the meaning of the scriptures to address life challenges.

I recommend this inspirational book to readers who want to resolve life struggles through a closer alignment with the presence and mind of God."

Dr. Robert J. Williams, Jr., MPH, Vice Chairperson, Board of Trustees, Bridge Street AWME Church.

★★★

"Discover a journey of self-discovery, healing, and spiritual growth with 'Revelations for Resilience: Whispers from the Divine for Soul Care.' This heartfelt collection of devotions offers guidance, hope, and healing for those navigating life's challenges. Join AndreYAH on a path towards resilience and hope, and find inspiration and guidance for your personal growth journey."

Dr. Joseph Ige (PhD, EdD, DMin, DBA, DSc., MPH, FISDS)
President, Triumphant Christian University of America

★★★

"AndreYAH has been through a war, or perhaps several wars at the same time, including the flight of a loved one, the death of her beloved mother, and prejudices that seemed to come from every front. Her body could not withstand the assaults, and she developed Post Traumatic Stress Disorder as she attempted to fend off the pain. The severity of her condition almost destroyed her. Almost. Through the darkness of her nights, she retreated into the most comforting and powerful safety she could find, the loving, protective arms of God.

As AndreYAH recovered, she recorded her daily experiences with God in a journal. Those inner knowings are revealed in this book and demonstrate the personal, caring, and sustained presence of God in her life. Despite outward appearances, God was leading AndreYAH to her victories…the restoration of her health and the emergence of a newer, more stable, more successful AndreYAH, stronger than ever and certain she could withstand any challenge with the love and support of her God. Her quotations from scripture provide a summary for each day's journal entry, but it is her stream of consciousness discoveries, her poetic explanations of her journey, and her blessings from God that invite the reader to explore how an intimate relationship with God can be achieved and sustained."

Adrienne Sprouse, M. D.,
Medical Director-Manhattan Health Consultants, New York, NY.

"This book is exactly what we need in this society and in this day and time. As patients, pastors, professionals, youth, adults, counselors, and people of the everyday community, this book exposes us to the sensitivity we need to heal in today's world.

The insight shared allows the author to help us bathe in the expanding calmness of our souls and get in touch with the spirituality needed to survive through the turmoil of life. Thanks to the ideas pinpointed by the author, our spirits can expand our thinking, and life goals."

**Reverend Joyce Peebles,
Pastor, Chaplain, Practical Theological,
and Family Manager**

CONTENTS

A Personal Letter to Readers 7
Day 1: Keep Your Mind Fixed On Me 16
Day 2: Don't Touch My Anointed One ... 20
Day 3: Yahweh Speaks in Affliction 24
Day 4: The Lord is for Me 28
Day 5: Fear Not, I Am Here 31
Day 6: Suffering Shipwreck 35
Day 7: I'm Always for You 38
Day 8 : Escape and Renew 40
Day 9 : Rest from all the Cacophony 42
Day 10: I Already Knew You 45
Day 11: I Will Multiply You 47

Day 12: I Am With You 50
Day 13: I Never Left You 54
Day 14: Rejoice 57
Day 15: The Wonders Of Balance 60
Day 16: Finish The Race 62
Day 17: I Am Your Fortress 64
Day 18: Trust Me 67
Day 19: There Is A Season For Every Thing 69
Day 20: Run To Win 72
Day 21: Keep Your Mind Stayed On Me .. 74
Day 22: Don't Worry About Tomorrow ... 76

CONTENTS

Day 23: Don't Be Consumed 78

Day 24: I Am Your Counsel 80

Day 25: Take Care of Yourself 82

Day 26: Keep Up the Good Work 84

Day 27: A Stone that Hears 87

Day 28: Chiseled By Mercy 90

Day 29: You're an Overcomer 92

Day 30: You Became the Works of
My Hands 94

Final Words from the Author 96

Photo Credit: Angel Painting, Hilda Rank

―――

"Treat people the same way you want them to treat you." Luke 6:31. (NAS)

FROM MY HEART TO YOURS

—

A Personal Letter to My Readers

Dear Reader,

In the pages that follow, I open up a sacred part of my soul—an offering shaped by intimate conversations with God, expressed through the language of poetry and devotion…

In a turbulent season, the "Poet of Heaven-Yahweh/YHWH" spoke as I opened my soul to this sacred work. Yahweh reminded me of His covenant, His assurance—even in the midst of shipwreck. This book was born of tribulation—a time when divine words lifted me to higher spiritual frequencies. I offered my vulnerability to the Heavenly Father. Freely, in private, I danced with my whole heart expressing myself with golden flags before my King, releasing pain while holding on to His promises. These pages trace journeys over rivers and rocks, and weave tapestries from many cultures and experiences. Through shipwreck and in need of a new heart—like the Tin Man on his way to Oz—I faced unexpected storms. Yet sacred resilience hugged me tightly and never let go, even when the one who vowed his life and ringed my finger with flawless diamonds, vanished without regard.

The writings you'll read in this book are poetic revelations—like Egyptian paintings or hieroglyphs that come alive on a museum wall, quietly unveiling purity, raw vulnerability of various stories, and authenticity. They inject hope and healing straight into our veins. I pray these chapters bring confidence to all who have—or may one day—journey through the fiery furnace.

On one occasion, my late dear friend Judy said to me, "God is really real!" My living testimony leveled her thermometer of faith to a higher notch. I echo this not in boast, but as a reality shaped by the heart-wrenching moments of my personal journey—even when those I cherished abandoned me, and attempted to defame my name. In order to thrive through these invisible injuries, I placed my enormous faith in the hands of Yahweh. Time and time again, without fail, He caused me to prevail against odds that would have overpowered me without divine intervention.

Dear beloved readers, in 2016, when I first began my healing journey, I was clinically diagnosed with Post-Traumatic Stress Disorder (PTSD)—a mental health condition that can cause symptoms such as nightmares, flashbacks, surges of stress hormones like cortisol and adrenaline, anxiety, emotional distress, a racing heartbeat, and digestive discomfort, to name a few. While in therapy, the coping skills I gained were my aid in navigating the sting of this horrific trauma. Medication can be helpful for many, but some people like myself prefer a more holistic approach. As an alternative medicine practitioner for over 30 years, I found comfort and homeostasis in varied modalities such as reflexology, acupuncture, Chinese medicine, chiropractic, shiatsu, meditation and diagrammatic breathing, running track, a vegan diet and basking in nature. All of these modalities made me feel balanced and whole.

It took some time, but in cooperation with my relentless faith, my broken eagle wings were restored amazingly.

Many people assume PTSD only affects

veterans, yet countless others silently carry the weight of trauma from different predicaments in life. I am one of them. Often misunderstood—even in the most caring communities—we learn to protect our peace by stepping back from noise, tension, stress or anything that stirs up overwhelm or hyper-vigilance. It's not about avoiding life—it's about protecting and preserving self-value, homeostasis and feeling safe in spaces that lack empathy, or may sometimes feel too instrusive, too chaotic, or overstimulating.

For me, sounds above 80 decibels—crowded rooms, fireworks, gunshots, roaring vehicles, harsh frequencies, loud voices, and even argumentative folk—can send waves of panic and anxiety crashing through me. I had to remind myself that I am an alternative medicine practitioner, and to lean on my lifelines—deep breathing, grounding, mindfulness, aromatherapy and reflexology—to calm my spirit, while distancing myself from the negative energies I could control.

In 2019, I made the difficult choice to leave the "Big Apple." New York City was a city that had shaped much of my early artistic and wellness career, yet it no longer cared for my nervous system—or my need for peace and longevity.

Sometimes, loneliness creeps in quietly, without warning. Each day, we live with our emotions and memories—some tender, some explosive—capable of stirring deep waves of pain or unexpected sorrow. It's the kind of ache that can linger silently in the corners of our lives, even when we're surrounded by people.

For me, the safest place to release what I carried was in communion with the Lord—through prayer, journaling, and long, quiet walks in nature. I also found comfort in weekly therapeutic meetings with others who have endured similar pain, and within the four safe walls of my therapist's office, where I discovered not just understanding and compassion, but a steady kindness—the kind you find in a true friend.

In my wilderness season, I walked through valleys where loneliness seemed endless, fighting for hope amidst excruciating pain. In one barrel, I carried multiple losses—too many to name. Yet to mention a few: spousal abandonment; valuables stolen from my storage; the loss of confidantes such as my mother, godmother, and grandmothers who have passed; and other relatives who had been my seasoned pillars of sweet support. Each day, I urgently focused on the light at the end of the tunnel, moving through the valley of the shadow of death, guided by the faithful hand of my Heavenly Father~Yahweh.

Many people today desire a microwave fix, yet true healing cannot be rushed if we are to receive the full blessing of divine wisdom and growth—the kind that leads to personal resurrection. Thank God, the healing balm of Gilead met me daily. The Divine Comforter reminded me of the queen He created me to be, rekindling my will to live and fulfill my purpose. The Holy Spirit has been my closest friend for many years — my source of peace and clarity.

Through prayer, worship, and song, I found strength and renewal. In my darkest moments, that inner guidance became my anchor, helping me to stay grounded and whole — mentally, physically, financially, socially, and emotionally. Looking at my life today, I must say, I'm extremely proud of my progress and unwavering relationship with my Creator; it's one that no one could ever sever.

In 2017, I remember sharing my journey with one of my aunts, a seasoned, wise woman in her 90s who listened as I told my story. She then replied, "You'll be okay because you come from strong roots." I reflected on her words, and it's true—strength runs in my DNA, inherited from the Motherland, as well as my American Indian, and Spanish ancestry.

I thank God daily for my late mother, who laid a solid spiritual foundation for me in my early childhood. She valued and raised her four daughters with the utmost integrity and taught us how to become resilient.

In high school, I resided in Stamford, Connecticut, I became a member of an exciting Baptist church at the age of eleven and remained active there until I graduated. At church, I enjoyed baking cakes for bake sales and touring with the youth choir, where we sang at various churches across the Tri-State area.

One Sunday, I heard the Lord whisper to take the preacher's hand; it was then I began to turn my life around and received redemption. Later, in the vibrant heart of the church, I was baptized—immersed in the cool, cleansing waters of the pulpit pool, washing away the old and renewing my spirit for a new beginning. My family's pride was unmistakable as my mother, father, sisters, cousins, great-aunts, and grandmothers filled the pews. When I opened my eyes and looked up, I saw a pillar of light—signaling the start of a life firmly anchored in God.

As I entered my teenage years, a turning point came at a part-time job at a call center, where I met Maria, a college student. At sixteen, I was drawn to her vibrant faith. She shared the Word of God so openly that she invited me to a powerful and exciting Bible study in her home—where I was welcomed with love and met incredible women of God who offered sisterhood and poured into my life. That group of spiritually mature adults lit a fire in my heart to learn more about theology and a closer relationship with Yahweh. Maria discipled me with grace and generosity, even covering the cost for me to attend Bible school through her church. I believe God placed Maria in my life at the perfect season.

In 2014 my mother transitioned to glory; her spiritual legacy still lives on in me. Even in her absence, I could feel her presence reminding me, "I taught you everything you need to navigate in this world, and AndreYah, you know the LORD." And it was true—she had prepared me well. However, I still felt alone and missed her sound wisdom and care. I missed her lovely voice and physical presence, especially because I was suffering silently. Yet, in my lowest moments, it was my reliance on the supernatural balm of Gilead—again and again—who soothed my soul and pushed me onward and upward.

Furthermore, every morning during my healing journey in 2016, I set aside intentional quiet time to pray, reflect, and write. It became my spiritual medicine. I journaled the divine insights I received each day, and through that process, my mind was renewed and lifted to a higher frequency in God. I don't know what I would have done without daily communication with Him—it grounded me. These simple yet powerful practices became my anchor, helping me stay focused on my divine purpose.

Throughout that year, I wrote over 420 revelatory devotions. And in 2017, I sensed the instruction from Yahweh to publish 30 of them—for the healing and encouragement of others. Through much patience, I believe this is the appointed season to release my work into the world. Especially in this era, when empathy, justice, and kindness seem to be fading amidst the shadows of racism and violence, we desperately need divine guidance and Godly love to heal and restore our world. Yet change begins within each of us. Through renewed faith, unwavering hope, strong marriages, united families, and a return to a positive, community-focused mindset—rooted in courageous hearts and a commitment to our shared humanity—we can rebuild what has been broken and move forward together.

"Darkness cannot drive out darkness; only light can do that. Hate cannot drive out hate; only love can do that."—Dr. Martin Luther King, Jr.

As I come to the end of my letter, reflecting on this enriching journey of self-discovery grounded in faith and enhanced by alternative healing practices. I can say with joy that I've been beautifully reinvented. When we trust God through our darkest valleys, we emerge not just as thrivers, but as miracles in motion—transformed by divine love and rising into higher realms of enlightenment, where old paradigms fall away, replaced by God's promises and truth-filled self-talk.

I invite you to approach this book as a daily spiritual multivitamin—nourishing your spirit and soul with sacred whispers from Yahweh. Within these pages, you'll find wisdom, truth, encouragement, and a gentle call to realign with divine enlightenment, one day at a time.

As long as we draw breath, we have the chance to deepen our relationship with God—a relationship that has been my greatest source of strength and can be yours too, if it isn't already. Open your heart to experience the power, guidance, comfort, and forgiveness of our heavenly Father—Abwoon, Our Beloved Father-Mother of the Universe.

May His healing, wisdom, and love gently guide you on a transformative journey into unconditional grace.

These 30 devotions are heartfelt whispers from Yahweh, offering scriptures that enlighten and comfort your soul—not exhaustive theological lessons.

I truly believe these sacred words will lift your spirit and enfold you in a tender embrace, meeting you right where you are. Know that you are deeply and unconditionally loved by Yahweh/God, and under His wings, there is more than enough healing for you.

With grace, shalom, and love,

AndreYAH

DAY
01

"Thou wilt keep him in perfect peace, whose mind is stayed on thee: because he trusteth in thee."
Isaiah 26:3, (KJV)

Photo Credit:
A.M.H. Black, Personal
Retreat, Hyannis, Cape Cod

KEEP YOUR MIND FIXED ON ME

Canto 1: My Beloved, Child

I am Your Beloved Father ~*Abwoon—Father-Mother of the Universe*. I love you more than humankind could fathom.

I've collected your tears; each one was like a soft raindrop that safely fell frozen onto my hands.

Now, relax and let your face feel the warmth of the rays of sunshine.
Bask in the great galaxies of My love.
Keep your mind flowing in the perfect wind and rhythm of My Spirit.

Canto II: A Child's Journey

My child, I've observed your heart of loyalty toward Me.
Continue climbing up the heavenly stairway.
Come to our secret place to dine.
Let's drink and digest the holy fire of My divine revelation.

I love you, My precious jewel.

I am your sustenance, the very essence of your life.

Canto III: Designed with Purpose

Before the world was created,
I designed you with purpose—both for My delight, to uplift, and to serve a platter of charity to others.

Countless avenues await your footsteps, allowing you to showcase my glory through your testimonies and multiple gifts.

Continue offering graciousness to the underprivileged,
even as the pompous look down with noses held high.

Keep spreading your compassionate wings of love and kindness towards others; perhaps one day, they'll realize I'm real—just like you did.

Canto IV: Trials and Faith

Your essence speaks for itself.

The Good News you share reflects My image.

Beloved, bring hope to the thirsty and the unthirsty.

Remain rooted in Me, and you'll soar in every divine pursuit.

Remember, I consecrated you, knew you, and kissed you before you were in the sacred womb of your mother.

Canto V: The Battle Within

I revealed why so-called friends
sent daggers of persecution your way—
they resented the righteous lifestyle you chose.

You met evil at its worst.
I know you haven't faced envy and wickedness at such a high level—especially from the one who once vowed love to you.

Beloved, listen to me:
a worldly being who doesn't know Me or hasn't honored Me may struggle to sincerely love you.

My beloved, love doesn't abandon, persecute, abuse, defame, or wish ill!

The mind of humankind often battles with good and evil.

Canto VI: Clothed in Grace

Beloved, stay wrapped in the pure white garments
I've lovingly draped over you—symbols of grace, hope, and new beginnings.

I'm an unlimited God;
I created you to become boundless.

You're blessed immeasurably.

I am your Heavenly Father, who continues to restore all of what the canker-worm gobbled and stolen.

I know this tragedy has unraveled you to shock.

Yet, beloved, your crown is crystallizing and sparkling with multi-colored fine diamonds.

Don't look back, dear. You've triumphed from hell.

Remember, beloved, the world may abandon you, but I am incapable of abandoning My children.

Please don't let these wounds drag you into mental hellish entanglement.

In Me, beloved, is perfect shalom.

DAY
02

"Saying, Touch not touch mine anointed, and do my prophets no harm."
I Chronicles 16:22, (KJV)

Photo Credit:
A.M.H. Black, Personal
Martha's Vineyard, Cape Cod

DON'T TOUCH MY ANOINTED ONE

Canto I: My Beloved, Child

I saw you praying beneath the tallit—in quiet distress, yet holding on to the tzitzit.

When you've done all you can,
remain standing on the rock of deliverance.

My healing arms, like eagle's wings,
scooped you up and cradled you gently.
Woman of God—You are My precious baby.

Beloved, you remained steadfast—pure
and immersed in My love—even through excruciating persecution.

It's okay to cry—letting your tears fall is healing for your soul.
Tears are not weakness; you don't have to carry the weight of being invincible.

Canto II

Torrential waves, stormy seas, and the hurricanes of life tried to take you out, but never succeeded.

Remember My words:
"Vengeance is mine; I will repay."
You are safe—held securely in the palm of My hand.

The one who tried to extinguish your destiny
has not apologized, and as a result, brings vengeance upon themselves.

Canto III

Those who menaced you—strategically

placing their misleading pawns—were the very ones who lacked the courage to face you.
They hurled their daggers from a distance, leaving you starved and vulnerable.
Yet some stood astonished at how you survived the trials that were meant to break you.

You were submerged in a sea of overwhelming grief, yet you kept swimming through the deep waves.

Your faith in yourself never ran dry.
You fought to rise above the pain—wrestling day after day with the weight of post-traumatic stress.

Canto IV

Through it all, you remained bathed in worship,
riding out the bumpy midnight horrors of flashbacks.
I reminded you to return to your holistic practices—to restore balance to your sympathetic and parasympathetic systems—through diaphragmatic breathing, reflexology, massage, acupuncture, Chinese medicine, and a vegan diet.
You followed My guidance, and healing began—amazingly, without medications.

Canto V

Throughout your cyclonic season, you sought Me and professional counsel for healing.

You ran into the bosom of Abraham, where you were held close—like Saturn's rings circling endlessly, wrapping you in a radiant presence of love.
This love flowed through you, nurturing your spirit, your body—every cell, every spark of thought—restoring all that was weary.

Canto VI

You longed for loving arms to hold you, but none were available in your dire loneliness. Therefore, you sang to Me, as Whitney Houston sang: "I Look to You."

You sang to Me on Mount Kilimanjaro, "How Great Thou Art."

You sung, "Livin' My Life like it's Golden," as Jill Scott expressed.

You vowed that no one was allowed to come into your palace with a flagellum, so you sang and danced to,
"No More Drama," like Mary J Blige cried.

My ambassador, you never gave up.
My promise to heal you and cover you with grace
has always been a promise.

DAY
03

"He delivereth the poor in his affliction, and openeth their ears in oppression."
Job 36:15, (KJV)

Photo Credit:
A.M.H. Black,
Personal Retreat at Mohonk Mountains, Mohonk, NY

YAHWEH SPEAKS IN AFFLICTION

My Beloved, Child

Every day, your enemies seek to wrap
their tentacles of doubt, worry, torment, fear,
and confusion in your world, but those toxic
spirits have failed and will never succeed in
devouring you.

Like swirling smoke, their deception
circulates the tree of darkness and spews on
the pure.
They smile face to face, mocking, gossiping,
and laughing; as if their actions are unlike
switchblades.

They cheat without remorse, steal without
hesitation, lie as easily as they breathe—yet
still,
they have the nerve to condemn you for
your sacrality, as though your truth threatens
the comfort of their illusions.

Beloved, they don't have your best interests at
heart.

With enlightened eyes, you saw through
facades,
recognizing sincerity is no guarantee of truth.
Yet, your hands remain interlocked with
mine.

Your steadfastness makes your enemies angry.
They are disguised sheep covered with white
linen.

Their tongue, driven by envy,
produces misleading reports and defamation.
Believe nothing they utter.
Integrity is far from their demeanor.
It's good to know the authenticity of
charlatans.

According to the judge, their crimes were
theft, defamation, death threats, and severe

psychological abuse.
The judge issued an order of protection.
Now the one who betrayed you feels the sting of shame and embarrassment.

They hide behind the Cypress trees, unable to face the light you still carry.

Beloved, throughout the trauma,
you maintained a quiet eye and a discerning tongue.
You've kept your thoughts elevated to a celestial state.

Many evenings, I witnessed you lying prostrate and
praying for hours on your African lavender, pink and green prayer mat.
I dried your tears and fought your battles, many of which you never witnessed.
You didn't shrink or drown;
you stood for justice.

You, soaked in green pastures where My love was plush.
I revitalized your soul and strengthened you for your new chapter.
When I lifted you up and cuddled you, you melted in my arms, but after some mending, you flew like an eagle.

Today, Beloved, I'm asking you to adopt a more elevated stance,
which is to keep praying for those who think ill of you.
You can only do this via me.

You are anointed, and My supernatural power is upon you.
Only the ones who have learned to rise from the depths of despair can intercede for their foes.

Like your earthly Daddy said,
"One bad apple won't stop, no show."

DAY 04

"The Lord shall fight for you, while you keep silent."
Exodus 14:14, (NASB)

Photo Credit:
Pavel Antonov,
Battery Park, Manhattan, NY

THE LORD IS FOR ME

My Beloved, Child

I've fought many battles you didn't see.

Gallows were set up to snare you, like the one Haman built for Mordecai.

The malevolent soul who harbored envy and hunted you down has now stumbled into the very snare set for you.
That vessel tried to use rotten shenanigans to slaughter you, yet their evil attempt backfired.

Their vices were strangled in a blazing flame. Enlightened ones often prize silence.

However, they are cognizant of tormenting wolves who paint themselves as ghosts in white gowns.

The foolish speak words that leave scarlet stains, unaware of their precious light.

Such a soul longs for love but envy the pure; so they sleep and reap misery.
Their deadly tentacles of muddy cistern scream; they are unwilling to repent. They conjure crimes targeting the innocent and the enlightened.

The pearls you once trusted around their neck, I've removed.

They mocked you behind blackout curtains, thinking no one would ever view their countenance, yet your eyes beheld clarity, and you proceeded strategically with wisdom.

I rejoice in your steadfastness. You never deserved this treatment, nor did the ancient elders of old, who faced injustice, enslavement, brutality, forced labor, debt bondage, rape, shipwrecks, auctions, and lynchings.

The wicked couldn't see My wings protecting you. They're confused now because your heart is still beating.

You're transforming, and soaring higher than eagles. You are in this world, but not of its wickedness.

You are in Me, for Me, and never turned against Me. You live in My bosom, dear child.

Continue to carry the scintillating torch of integrity that your forefathers proudly marched with.

Stand victorious with your armor on; hold the holy sword in the palm of your right hand.

Yes, I've kept you elevated—sheltered beneath My tent My love—hidden from the destructive forces that rose against your righteousness. They tried to engulf you, but yes, they've failed…

When you sing "This Little Light of Mine" — the Civil Rights Movement song — to your audiences…sing that same song to yourself.

My message to you is this: your light is not small; it is a great light within you.

Let it thrive.

DAY
05

"Even from eternity I am He, And there is no one who can rescue from My hand; I act, and who can reverse it?"
Isaiah 43:13, (NASB)

Photo Credit:
A.M.H. Black,
**Mohonk Mountains,
Mohonk, NY**

FEAR NOT, I AM HERE

My Beloved, Child

I am Yahweh (YHWH/God), who is Faithful and True.

In the courtroom, even the judge was astounded by the malicious defamation of false documents
signed by an individual who sought to persecute and abandon you.
The documents were fabricated signatures by your enemies pretending to be great leaders who wanted to entomb you.

Masked familiar faces were uncovered as foes.
Jealousy is as ferocious as the grave.
Envy stems from its inability to defeat the glory within My people.

Success eluded the wicked ones, leaving them incapable of achieving victory over you.

Contrary to their wishes, you defied death and excelled.

I am for you, My child, never against you. Keep your hand in mine; together, we conquer.

You were sure that your close associates and kin
would exemplify unconditional love and support.
Yet some, unable to fully grasp the pain and challenges of your condition,
struggled to respond with understanding, some lacked compassion…

Beloved, I'm sorry that others have faltered.
I made humans to foster friendship and familial bonds,
rather than isolation or to succumb to hyper-independence.

On one hand, you could count the fewer-than-five priceless souls who embraced you. They were the radiant ones—gentle in spirit, sincere in kindness, and with open arms.

My child, I am a constant friend; my arms can't stop hugging you.

I understand how difficult it was to cope with the pain of abandonment, while experiencing restlessness and flashbacks in the wee-hours.
My love, I was the one who soothed your concerns.
I comforted your mind to finally fall asleep.

Beloved, I remember one day at the University,
when your symptoms began to flare, and you felt exhausted from the long haul.
You contemplated giving up the fight more than once—but My reassuring revelation came,
like hope, soothing you to live on, gently saving your life.

Now, look at you!

You're soaring in new chapters and living victoriously.
Continue to elevate beyond galaxies!

Beloved, sometimes, the miracle antidote is a process—much like the time it takes for the sun to rise and set, or for the earth to revolve around the sun.

Throughout your arduous journey,
I, Yahweh, your Almighty Father,
remained steadfastly by your side,
even when you succumbed
to the overwhelming suffering
outside the sacred edifice.

Remember, victory is your name,
and defeat will never claim you.
As a testament to this sacred bond,
associates, friends, and even former adversaries
cannot deny the existence of our divine covenant.

This is one of your greatest testimonies!

My child, I held you tightly in my arms,

offering unwavering support through your most challenging days, even when the one who vowed to love you forever — the one who placed that brilliant diamond upon your finger — vanished.

My dear, the mind that conjured recipes of evil and envy truly inflicted misery on himself,
losing sight of the blessings I had graciously bestowed upon him.

Dear heart, you have lost nothing.

Yes, I felt the pain when the perfect puzzle of your heart shattered into a million pieces.
I promised to mend you and I lifted you to triumph—now and throughout eternity.

There is nothing to fear in this macrocosm.

Whether friend, foe, kin, or politician,
no force outside ourselves can ever break the extraordinary covenant we share;
its resilience remains unyielding.

DAY 06

"Three times I was beaten with rods, once I was stoned, three times I was shipwrecked, a night and a day I have been in the deep."
2 Corinthians 11:25, (NKJV)

Photo Credit:
Almetra Murdock,
AndreYah Speaker at Retreat, Topsails, NC

SUFFERING SHIPWRECK

—

My Beloved, Child

My voice sounds like a thousand waves louder than ships' torrential torment at sea, and yet, you still heard Me.

When the harmonious yet dissonant waves thrust you into shock—I stood with you, remember?
I stood with you, remember?
I carried you safely in My right hand.

Also, do you remember that day—waiting for the bus in Allegheny County?
I saw you collapse on the grass before the church,
your eyes and arms lifted as you shouted My name—longing to be raptured.

The shock of abandonment electrocuted your soul with a blazing fire of torment beyond words.

It took three years to heal from the phases of your invisible wounds.
Your therapist offered you steady tools—to navigate grief, multiple losses, and trauma.
Yet I was your soul's source and faithful partner, providing daily miracles along your journey.

You longed for your trusted confidant—your mother of late, who understood you better than anyone.
I know you miss mom — her lovely voice still speaks to your spirit.
She was your unconditional friend in the flesh, even shielding you with comforting words of the ancestors, as an African "Mama" hen would.

Your Father's loving voice comforted you, encouraging you to begin a new chapter.
You remained safe in His gentle care, even as

your enemies mocked you from their hidden caves.

I was your spiritual guide—holding you close to my heart and understanding you beyond words.

Keep climbing toward the mountaintop. Even the steepest paths can be reached by the courageous.

My dearest, I call you Makeda—your spirit wears triumph like a majestic queen.

I take delight in you, for you live in My glorious image.

DAY 07

"What shall we then say to these things? If God be for us, who can be against us?"
Romans 8:31, (KJV)

Photo Credit:
Alexandre Neishtadt,
Respite in Silver Bay, Lake George, NY

I'M ALWAYS FOR YOU

My Beloved, Child

You poured a cup of living water
for the fractured soul of Jekyll and Hyde,
while darkness clawed your edges.

Through the trembling tunnel of shadows of death's dark valley,
you lifted your eyes to My face;
you felt awakened to heaven's wisdom.

Your quest for wholeness became your offering;
step by step, you pressed urgently into new dimensions of shalom and became restored.
Your face began to shine, like Moses—
who experienced radiance when he spoke to Me.

In your quiet moments of worship, prayer, and fasting,
your heart and ears were wide open,
tuning in to astounding visions.

Beloved, if I am for you, who in this world can be against you?

Day
08

"Come unto me, all ye that labour and are heavy laden, and I will give you rest. Take my yoke upon you, and learn of me; for I am meek and lowly in heart: and ye shall find rest unto your souls. For my yoke is easy, and my burden is light."
Matthew 11:28-30, (KJV)

Photo Credit:
A.M.H. Black,
Hiking in Kent Falls, CT

ESCAPE AND RENEW

My Beloved, Child

It's high time for a getaway.

Relieve yourself of city toxicity, crowds, train shrieks, noisemakers, motorcycles, loud talking, and eternal sirens.

Escape the clamor and chaos.
Immerse yourself in green earth—inhale solace and homeostasis.

Let's connect deeper.

In nature's quiet embrace,
your spirit is renewed—refreshed and filled with life once more.

My Beloved, even your cells and neurons rejoice, awakened and revitalized.

DAY 09

"He giveth power to the faint; and to them that have no might he increaseth strength."
Isaiah 40:29 (KJV)

Photo Credit:
Almetra Murdock,
Fred G Bond Metro Park, Cary, NC

REST FROM ALL THE CACOPHONY

My Beloved, Child

Maintain a deep and sacred connection with the Holy Spirit; allow Me to be your guide—divine and infinite.

In the quiet of both natural and realms unseen,
let us savor our fellowship—pure and serene.

I have given you mountains and seas to explore—
for soul care, for delight, and communion forevermore.

I've given power and might— to steward the Earth with reverence and right.

Obey My instructions while you walk this land;
keep your heart near Mine, and always hold My hand.

Do not despise small beginnings or days that seem slow— they are seeds of a harvest that you'll come to know.

No longer will you grieve dead leaves;
Keep bathing in the fountain of My living hot springs.

Allow Me to cleanse you with hyssop for the journey.

You're an olive tree branching out.

It's your season!

You've been resilient like Cedars of Lebanon.

I am the same Lord your ancestors believed, they trusted in Me and were never deceived.

Bask in shalom, let peace make you free—
this supernatural power extends longevity.

Hold fast your habits of care and repair,
don't let your spirit fall into despair.

My Beloved, come and rest your mind, let
your spirit be adorned and refined, clothed
in the royal robes Queen Esther once
wore—ones ordained to be respected and
adored.

DAY 10

"Before I formed thee in the belly I knew thee, and before thou camest forth out of the womb I sanctified thee; I have appointed thee a prophet unto the nations."
Jeremiah 1:5 (ASB)

Photo Credit:
A.M.H. Black,
**Mohonk Mountains,
Mohonk, NY**

I ALREADY KNEW YOU

My Beloved, Child

I knew you before you were formed within your mother's womb, and saw the person you were meant to be—beyond others' limitations.

Soar like an eagle, fearless and free.

You've sat at the feet of your seers—your late ancestors: mother, father, great-aunts, and grandmothers—of indigenous bloodlines, heirs of divine intuition, wisdom, and revelation.

You've always been an old soul.

Keep pouring into those with ears to hear and hearts to receive.

Though the know-it-alls may turn away, share your wisdom freely, touching hearts everywhere—even those not yet seeking.

Remember, I have placed people in your path
to honor and celebrate the fullness of who I made you to become.

Never forget—your validation comes from Me alone, not from the fleeting judgments of others.

Remember that your mother and father instilled in you—integrity, perseverance, faith, confidence and generosity—they reside in your royal legacy.

DAY 11

"Behold, I will make thee fruitful, and multiply thee, and I will make of thee a multitude of people; and will give this land to thy seed after thee for an everlasting possession."
Genesis 48:4, (KJV)

Photo Credit:
A.M.H. Black,
Meditating at Seaside Park, Bridgeport, CT

I WILL MULTIPLY YOU

My Beloved, Child

It's sunrise, your heart begins to sing,
Let's walk by the ocean where shalom is king.
Meditate, breathe, and commune with Me,
In stillness and love, where your spirit is free.

Keep your goals close, work smart and remain true,
trust your voice and the wisdom in you.
Though many doubt the Ancient of Days,
their spirit thrives because they follow My ways.

When life seems unclear, walk steady and bright,
Take the first step, guided by love and light.

As a child, you were set to be multiplied,
With elders' wisdom always near your bedside.

Aligned with My Spirit, your path is clear;
your gifts given before time drew near.
Walk upright despite curious eyes,
Or scorn from those unkind and unwise.

I pour out My shalom, pure and whole.
Restoring your body, soul, and goals.
Take care of yourself, find strength in Me,
Mercy and forgiveness will always set you free.

Proclaim My love to the lost and worn,
Hope is renewed and forever reborn.

My Son, the anointed one: **Isho the M'shiha** ~ (ܐܠܗܐ ܝܫܘ).

He came to restore all to wholeness and grace.
Isho (ܝܫܘܥ), M'shiha/Yeshu (יֵשׁוּעַ), Ha Massaich—His love and power will never

weaken your place.

The remnant call Him Iesous = Jesus (Ιησούς) or Yeshu (יֵשׁוּ).
Regardless of the name they pray—I know they worship me in spirit and truth.

My compassion is evident for those who see and believe.
Continue following My way of love, and receive.

DAY 12

"Teaching them to observe all things whatsoever I have commanded you: and, lo, I am with you alway, even unto the end of the world. Amen."
Matthew 28:20 (KJV)

Photo Credit:
A.M.H. Black,
Personal Retreat, Silver Bay on Lake George, NY

I AM WITH YOU

My Beloved, Child

As the dawn breaks,
I find you gracefully seated by the lake,
immersed in the splendor of nature, yet
in conversation with Me—your thoughts
drifting upon the tranquil waters.

Let your thoughts absorb the stellar energies
of the shimmering lake—the gentle waves,
the azure sky, fluffy clouds, towering
oaks, plush gardens, melodious birds, and
quacking ducks.

Nature is adorned in regal elegance.

My child, I cherish your visits with Me in nature,
for they have deepened our bond.

My heavenly Father, let's sit under the silky sky and by the sails on the lake.

What soothing tranquility.
LORD, I cherish our walks and hikes;
I relish the deep bond we share in communion.

My LORD, in revelatory fellowship, I love that our connection grows even stronger.

You're my everything!

Beloved, Father~Mother~Abwoon, you are perfect.

I cherish our laughter and enlightened dialogue.

Beloved child, your prayers and cries are like frankincense and myrrh.
I attend to every one of your concerns.

You're very inquisitive; I love that!

My lovely child, nature captivates you with balance and calm.
You are part of it, beautifully intertwined with all I created.

Remember, I crafted the galaxies, the stars, and the sun.

I'm the immeasurable frequency of sound beyond comprehension.

I declared: "Let there be light."

Beloved, life is full of roses, yet not full of roses…

Sometimes, you will have one rose of a friend, and one day, not even one. Indeed, humankind can be fleeting, but not Me.

One thing, My dearest heart is that I'll never forsake you.

Beloved, remember, I caused you to overcome cobras!

You've encountered unexpected thorns on your side, but with your hand in mine, you'll fly beyond the Milky Way.

My dear, you've relied on me for everything in the past; know that I'm incapable of ever failing you.

Now, close your eyes; meditate on the vibrant tapestry of my presence.

Allow Me to guide you into new strategies and heights of joy, beauty and generational wealth.

Rest in My shalom—the complete fullness that is beyond comprehension.

I never left you, dear child; you are soaring!

Thank You, dear Heavenly Father, for Your encouragement and guidance.
I am grateful for Your constant presence in my life.

DAY 13

"The eyes of the Lord are in every place, beholding the evil and the good."
Proverbs 15:3 (KJV)

Photo Credit:
A.M.H. Black,
Personal Retreat, Mohonk, NY

I NEVER LEFT YOU

My Beloved, Child

As you retreat to the Mohonk Mountains,
you feel the weight and grief of the injustices
suffered by your indigenous ancestors.

Even on US soil today, instability and despair
hang heavy.
The blood is on their hands;
I see it all with a grieving heart.
Their bread is greed;
they refuse to repent.

Since the beginning of time, I have entrusted
My indigenous with the duty of diligence—
to care for the land, and they did.

It was stolen!
Since the confiscation and massacre—the
sacred responsibility died in the grave.
Now the soil groans in endless anguish,
ravaged by hurricanes and shattered by
earthquakes.

Evil has no remorse and refuses to repent.
Greed and injustice continues to rage.

Remember, the book of Esther?
Read it again; there is a great lesson there.

Can greed come up higher and sow seeds of
justice?
Will they allow pride to rob them of fairness,
truth and compassion for the world?

The question is: Who is willing…
Not, who is not willing.

In arrogance, some earthlings seek to usurp
My throne, yet they fail themselves and face
their own demise alone.

Stand firm, keep the faith, and continue to

pray.
Some say that prayer is a waste of time, not so…

For what seems improbable to humanity is indeed achievable when aligned with My divine will.

Individuals who seek repentance, and follow My guidance with unwavering dedication will know My presence.

Will the one who desires injustice expect their sins to be forgiven?

Do they even realize their sin?
First let them repent, and then My true forgiveness will follow.
I am the ultimate arbiter of justice—merciful and wise.

DAY 14

"Rejoice in the Lord alway: and again I say, Rejoice."
Philippians 4:4 (KJV)

Photo Credit:
A.M.H. Black,
Respite in Silver Bay, Lake George, NY

REJOICE

My Beloved, Child

Rejoice, rejoice, rejoice, O beloved child of Zion!

Each day, regardless of your circumstances, find joy; remember to choose your battles wisely.

My Beloved, I fought many of your battles; even the ones you never thought existed.

Continue to stand with both feet planted on the rock of deliverance.

Do your part, and I'll do mine.

Some folk thought you'd give up, but that's not your name.
My child, your name is Faith, Hope, Courageous and Victory.

You'll never forget who you are—your roots run deep from your spiritual upbringing.

You have nothing to fear.
I am in you, with you, and you are in Me!
Do not use the word failure; instead, see life as feedback.
Applied feedback allows you to soar with new strength and wisdom.

Hold fast to My promises, no matter what others think, do, or say.
Fight with the sword of the Spirit—armed with prayer and hope.

Your name is Resilience.

Again, remain in your truth, regardless of scowling faces, rolling eyes, or tongues of defamation.

You are deeply loved, chosen, and destined for greatness.

Let your light shine—your story is not over.
You are My ambassador—sent to the nations.

You were betrayed, yet never conform to lower realms, nor waste your time on hate — instead, keep flying higher than eagles.

Don't allow the sun to spiral into a hollow barrel of disappointment or delays.

O, beloved, rejoice, rejoice, and lift your gaze!

Each prayer and every effort makes a difference.
You're a catalyst for change in the world.

Your presence is significant.

My Lord, and dearest, heavenly Father,

Sheol came for me, but it didn't win.
It tried to steal my will to live and my purpose,
but it never won; I won!
It never robbed me of My covenant with you; and it never will.

I hear you, dear child.
Rejoice! O, My precious, child of Zion, rejoice!

You know what, My dear beloved child?

My love for you is immeasurable!

Rise!

DAY 15

"Hearken unto this, O Job: stand still, and consider the wondrous works of God. Dost thou know when God disposed them, and caused the light of his cloud to shine? Dost thou know the balancings of the clouds, the wondrous works of him which is perfect in knowledge?"
Job 37-14-6 (KJV)

Photo Credit:
A.M.H. Black,
Respite in Hyannis, Cape Cod

THE WONDERS OF BALANCE

My Beloved, Child

You have immersed yourself in the embrace of nature; it has rejuvenated both your spirit and physical being.

I designed nature as a healing balm for humanity.

As you immerse yourself in its wonders this week, keep in mind that you're enhancing your cellular health and fortifying your immune system.
You really need this, especially after all you've endured.

The negative ions and antioxidants found in the natural world are mending and safeguarding your cells—fostering your overall well-being.

I crafted nature to harmonize your body's rhythms, to nurture vitality and healing.

Release the old, and breathe in the new; nature's vibrating energy fosters clarity and longevity.

DAY 16

"Know ye not that they which run in a race run all, but one receiveth the prize. So run, that ye may obtain."
1 Corinthians 9:24 (KJV)

Photo Credit:
A.M.H. Black,
Walking in Fred G. Bond Metro Park, Cary, NC

FINISH THE RACE

My Beloved, Child

Remain intentional and focused.
Do not become distracted by the world.

Remain in your divine and unique lane.

Your destiny is filled with gemstones.
Get past the endangered daggered cliffs and back-stabbers you've encountered.

You're an overcomer!
I have anointed you with power that the world could never give.

Your face and essence glimmers like pure gold.

Maintain your role as a beacon of integrity in all your endeavors.
Keep running strategically toward the finish line.
Run with grace and faithfulness—and claim your prize.

My love, I chose you first;
you did not choose yourself — you simply fell in love with Me and accepted your call and My covenant.

Courage, righteousness, and obedience will carry you to victory.

I see you lifting your eyes, recognizing My presence, illuminating beyond the clouds.

DAY
17

"I cried unto thee, O LORD: I said, Thou art my refuge and my portion in the land of the living."
Psalm 142:5 (KJV)

Photo Credit:
A.M.H. Black,
Respite in Hyannis, Cape Cod, MA

I AM YOUR FORTRESS

My Beloved, Child

I hear your cry, loud and clear.
You've even awakened and rumbled the ocean waves.

Yes, you can count on Me; I'm your fortress.

Do you hear me, beloved child?

Continue to trust Me in every endeavor, not just in some.

I will continue to upgrade your portions.
My favorable answers are far beyond your request.

Am I not the God of more than enough ~ "God Almighty" is (ܐܲܠܵܗܵܐ ܫܲܕܲܝ) Alaha Shaddaya?

You have received an overflow of My favor, get ready for harvest!

Take one step at a time.
Do not become fatigued by circumstances you haven't control of.

Every victorious woman; must pause to meditate, listen to her heart and embrace her beauty.
She must continue to be guided by the divine.
For her divine voice is within.

Continue walking with Me in spirit and truth.

Wealth, abundance, shalom, and profound insight are blossoming in your garden, reminiscent of the Rose of Sharon.

I am your refuge,
and My devotional fragrance surrounds you: spikenard, cinnamon, cassia, aloe, calamus, and myrrh.

DAY
18

"Trust in the LORD with all thine heart; and lean not unto thine own understanding. In all thy ways acknowledge him, and he shall direct thy paths."
Proverbs 3:5-6 (KJV)

Photo Credit:
A.M.H. Black,
Bridgeport, Connecticut

TRUST ME

My Beloved, Child

Though the road was dark and rough, you placed your trust in Me.

Your arms were lonely branches in the winter, yet you flourished like pomegranate trees.

You emerged stronger, lovelier and as bright as the Sombrero Galaxy.

What you endured, humankind could never fathom.

You are not the same person you were a year ago—you have grown in copious ways.

Had you relied on your own understanding, you would have sunk. But you trusted in Me, your Lord—I am glad you did.

I love you beyond the cosmos, My beloved child.

DAY 19

"To every thing there is a season, and a time to every purpose under the heaven: A time to be born, and a time to die; a time to plant, and a time to pluck up that which is planted; A time to kill, and a time to heal; a time to break down, and a time to build up; A time to weep, and a time to laugh; a time to mourn, and a time to dance; A time to cast away stones, and a time to gather stones together; a time to embrace, and a time to refrain from embracing; A time to get, and a time to lose; a time to keep, and a time to cast away; A time to rend, and a time to sew; a time to keep silence, and a time to speak; A time to love, and a time to hate; a time of war, and a time of peace."
Ecclesiastes 3:1-8, KJV

Photo Credit:
A.M.H. Black,
Respite, Hyannis, Cape Cod, MA

THERE IS A SEASON FOR EVERYTHING

My Beloved, Child

I have filled your mouth with the miracle oil of divine utterance.

A season exists for a moment for quietude.

There's a time to reflect and a time to observe.

You confused your enemies with your stillness of silence, yet when you spoke, your words held strength.

You've seen both the virtuous and the vile, yet no words are necessary,
for your observations have conveyed the truth.

You turned the page as your father advised; now you're flying.

All those days you and I sat together in nature and by your bedside,
I was infused with your profound enlightenment.

Dear child, what may matter to you, others may not value.

Yet stand firm, and keep proclaiming the Good News—for in time, it may lift others...

Always remain in your anointing;
when you do, you'll reflect Me.

Remember, there's a time to cry,
a time to laugh, and a time to put the old away.
That old chapter is gone dear;
refuse to go back.
Embrace your brand-new trajectory.

A Semitic poet put it this way:
"Back of the mill is the wheat and the sower, and the sun, and YHWH's will."

DAY 20

"Brethren, I count not myself to have apprehended: but this one thing I do, forgetting those things which are behind, and reaching forth unto those things which are before, I press toward the mark for the prize of the high calling of God in Christ Jesus."
Philippians 3:13-14 (KJV)

Photo Credit:
A.M.H. Black,
Hudson Valley, NY

RUN TO WIN

My Beloved, Child

Keep your focus on the good in your life.

Look not to the person beside you—
or to the one on your right or left.
Comparison steals one's balance,
and robs them of their beauty, value and destiny.

Remember, I designed each DNA uniquely;
you were meant to thrive in the shine I put in you.

You've never compared yourself to others.
Continue to embrace the phenomenal woman I've created you to become.

Those who are stuck and entangled in the world's web of identity—need you.

Strive daily to be a better version of yourself.

Furthermore, continue to study; this way, you won't fall into religion, embedded theologies, strongholds, deception, or false doctrines.

Above all, you know My voice,
just as your ancestors did.

Continue listening…

DAY 21

"Thou wilt keep him in perfect peace, whose mind is stayed on thee: because he trusteth in thee."
Isaiah 26:3 (KJV)

Photo Credit:
A.M.H. Black,
Hudson Valley, NY

KEEP YOUR MIND STAYED ON ME

My Beloved, Child

Express your zeal with fervor.
Go tell it on the mountain;
across the seas, valleys, and everywhere.

Continue on the straight and narrow.

Conquerors are ambassadors who rise and grow
from obstacles along the way.

I celebrate your accomplishments; greater exploits you will do.

Your testimonies inspire others to take risks;
perhaps they too may fall in love with Me, as you did.

The standards of others are not your key—
only My statutes.

Continue to condone toxic voices,
they're out of alignment with your destiny.

My everlasting love for you is forever, even when mistakes arise.

DAY
22

"Therefore do not worry about tomorrow, for tomorrow will worry about its things. Sufficient for the day is its trouble."
Matthew 6:34. (KJV)

Photo Credit:
A.M.H. Black,
Studying for exams, Bridgeport, CT

DON'T WORRY ABOUT TOMORROW

My Beloved, Child

Tones of red, orange, and yellow rise slowly; it's a day of excellence in your misty season.

Awake, kneel and commune with Me.
You may stop weeping now.

Stay focused today on objectives, and create deadlines; visualize accomplishing every goal.
Imagine what accomplishing today's goals feels like!

Beloved, you've been working over time.
It's time for a break!

Stretch, exercise, inhale deeply, and exhale slowly.
Walk in the air around the neighborhood.

I am your God, Alaha Shaddaya (ܐܠܗܐ ܫܕܝ).

My Dear, I have empathy and know that all you valued was stolen.

I promise to multiply it back to you, beyond your comprehension.

DAY 23

"No soldier on service entangles himself with the affairs of civilian life, so that he may please him who enlisted him as a soldier."
2 Timothy 2:4 (ASB)

Photo Credit:
A.M.H. Black,
Fred G. Bond Metro Park, Cary, NC

DON'T BE CONSUMED

My Beloved, Child

Many are addicted to greed and never satisfied,
entangled in the snares of recognition, power, and prestige. But yours—clothed in faith and truth—will not be swayed by their empty pursuits.

Don't be fooled by cheshire cat smiles; behind their backs, their hands hold daggers and defamation.

Pay them no mind—instead, rise!

Reach for the galaxies on High,
and keep stepping until victory is won.

My perfect guidance walks with you through eternity.

Keep going higher!

DAY 24

"For unto us a child is born, unto us a son is given: and the government shall be upon his shoulder: and his name shall be called Wonderful, Counsellor, The mighty God, The everlasting Father, The Prince of Peace."
Isaiah 9:6 (KJV)

Photo Credit:
A.M.H. Black,
Respite hiking in Silver Bay, Lake George, NY

I AM YOUR COUNSEL

My Beloved, Child

You haven't been forsaken; you're never alone.
In My presence, you'll find strength of your own.

I am your partner in all you pursue,
guiding each step, making all things new.

When you stumbled, still you rose again;
you sought My face for a better way,
and no one could ever lead you astray.

My word is your fortress, like shelter in storm;

I've been the Prince of Shalom before you were born.

I know every hair that rests on your head;
with grace and with hope, your spirit's always fed.

I am the protective Father and nurturing Mother—Abwoon.

Allow the government to remain upon My shoulders, not yours.

DAY 25

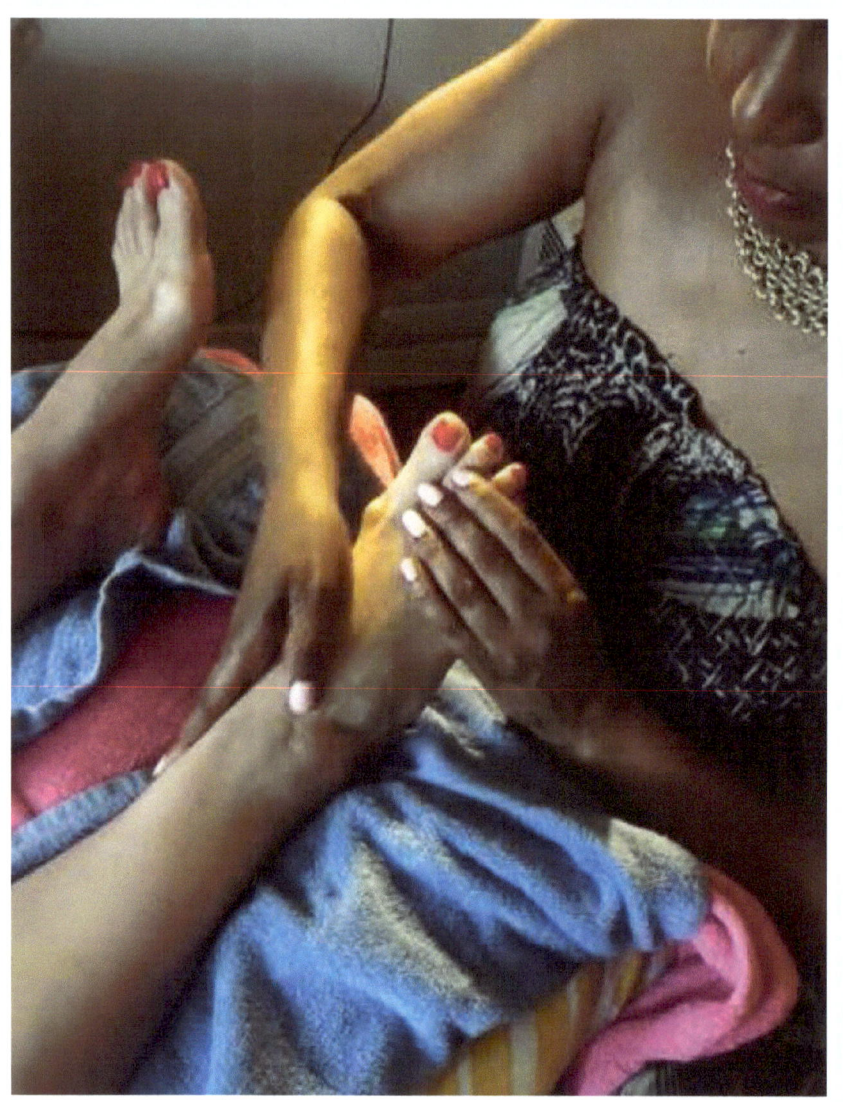

"Beloved, I wish above all things that thou mayest prosper and be in health, even as thy soul prospereth."
3 John 1:2 (KJV)

"The doctor of the future will give no medicine but will instruct his patient in the care of the human frame, in diet, and in the cause and prevention of disease."
—*Thomas Edison*

Photo Credit:
A.M.H. Black,
Ministering Foot Reflexology, Bronx, NY

TAKE CARE OF YOURSELF

—

My Beloved, Child

Continue to use your gift of alternative medicine,
healing yourself as you have healed others.

Your wellness treatments have offered miracles and longevity throughout the years.

Praying for your clients ignites the soul, guided by your mastery of reflexology and aromatherapy.

This essence of healing is in your hands; it's a gift from Me.

This is a calming fit for your hands and heart,
while desk-bound vocations have filled you with stress and anxiety.

Working in this field your spirit finds ease;
your work brings miracles.

Remember, your late grandmother Mama's final message was— every simple, yet so profound:
"Take care of yourself and be good to yourself."

DAY 26

"Come to him, a living stone, though rejected by mortals yet chosen and precious in God's sight, and like living stones, let yourselves be built into a spiritual house, to be a holy priesthood, to offer spiritual sacrifices acceptable to God through Jesus Christ."
1 Peter 2:4-5 (NRSV)

Photo Credit:
A.M.H. Black,
**Women's Wellness Retreat,
Garrison Institute, Garrison, NY**

KEEP UP THE GOOD WORK

My Beloved, Child

This is a quiet place to meditate; take a seat.

You've navigated many tumultuous predicaments, often alone.

I remember when you lived in Moscow after the Gulf War; you stood up for justice despite the predicaments you encountered.

Many in your family were unaware of the trials you endured there, or the fires that forged you into a regal warrior — like your ancestors.

Though it appeared you were alone, the strength you carried was the legacy passed down by the queens and kings who nourished you.

They've empowered you to fight for what is right.

Remember, what your mother declared in her final days? "It's how you finish, not how you start."

Beloved, as your wise uncle mentioned, "Not everyone has your best interest in mind."

Remain steadfast in humility.

The eagle-anointed eyes of the Great Spirit; will continue to reveal the truth from falsehood to you.

I, the Lord your God/Yahweh, called you before the world was formed;

I destined you, My dear, to become a holy nation.

Keep up the excellent work you're doing.

I long to say, "Well done, good and faithful servant."

Embrace the fullness of who I created you to become.

Amid your storms, your victories reflect My glory.

DAY 27

"To whom coming, as unto a living stone, disallowed indeed of men, but chosen of God, and precious, Ye also, as lively stones, are built up a spiritual house, an holy priesthood, to offer up spiritual sacrifices, acceptable to God by Jesus Christ."
1 Peter 2:4 (KJV)

Photo Credit:
A.M.H. Black,
Global Citizens Alliance Seminar Fellowship, Salzburg, Austria

A STONE THAT HEARS

My Beloved, Child

Continue to trust My divine revelation.
Heed to My voice and visions.

My spirit has brought you comfort—take relief, and do not worry.

In this season of rejoicing, I am broadening your horizons beyond galaxies.

Continue to declare my promises and righteous words over yourself.

It is My duty to guide My children and prepare them for their next phase,

yet some will not drink consecrated waters, but I know you will.

During your tumultuous season of coping with PTSD,
I inspired you to return—victoriously back to the University to advance your degree.

I know this journey wasn't easy.
Yet, by listening to My guidance,
you soared on the wings of graceful eagles, as I knew you would.

Remember when you submitted your essay for the Global Alliance Seminar Fellowship?

I whispered into your heart that you would become a recipient, inviting you to rest instead of worry. Quietly, you began to pack and prepare, filled with confidence, knowing you were headed to Austria—where mountain peaks glistened, dressed in pristine snow, awaiting your arrival.

My child, always keep your ear upon My heart.
My promises and revelation will always relieve you of worry, fear, and doubt.

DAY 28

"For we are His workmanship, created in Christ Jesus for good works, which God prepared beforehand that we should walk in them."
Ephesians 2:10 (KJV)

Photo Credit:
A.M.H. Black,
Personal Respite, Monhonk, NY

CHISELED BY MERCY

My Beloved, Child

You've been resurrected!
Your new strut of newness expands beyond human comprehension.

I am creating you as My masterpiece—like gold, refined in fire.

Beloved, you took My word and reinvented yourself.

Wow, some would say, "Who in the world could possibly rise from such a cataclysm?"

Beloved, look at you now, you're blossoming like a cypress tree!

You've taken your parents' advice well.

Throughout your journey, you've learned to put Me first, and everything else, thereafter.

Be very patient, for I am not finished with you yet.

DAY 29

"These things have I spoken to you, that in Me you may have peace. In the world you will have tribulation; but be of good cheer, I have overcome the world."
John 16:33 (KJV)

Photo Credit:
A.M.H. Black,
Hiking in Kent Falls, Kent, CT

YOU'RE AN OVERCOMER

My Beloved, Child

Through tears and steadfast vigilance,
you have endured and overcome great trials.
Take heart—for you live within My
everlasting arms.

You are My ambassador to the world.
Your name is Makeda.

You climbed triumphant ladders,
making wise decisions;
your comfort rests in the Holy Spirit.

When you were wrongly accused,
you stood firm, a soldier unshaken.

No one can derail your destiny.
My hand of oil rests firmly upon your head,
anointing you, sealing you,
for I ordained you an overcomer.

DAY 30

"So God created humans in his image, in the image of God he created them; male and female he created them."
Genesis 1:27 (KJV)

Photo Credit:
A.M.H. Black,
***Wedding Photo 2014,
Livingston, NJ***

YOU BECAME THE WORKS OF MY HANDS

My Beloved, Child

My dear, approach life one moment at a time.

I am your Beloved Father—all-knowing, ever-present, all-powerful; your Heavenly Father, Abwoon.

Some tried to tell you the Messiah never was,
yet you have seen Me.

You have witnessed the deaf hear, illnesses healed, people stepping into their true purpose—and that's just the beginning.

You have witnessed incredible transformations—blind eyes seeing again, legs regaining strength.
You have seen the deaf hear, illnesses healed, and people step into their true purpose, and that's just the beginning.

Yes, tell the doubters that I am real.

I am refining you into My masterpiece; continue to speak with Me about every single thing.

Keep your feet shod in the gospel of shalom.
I adore you beyond what you can fathom—
I will infinitely hold you tightly in My arms.

FINAL WORDS FROM THE AUTHOR

Dear Reader,

I'm so grateful that you've made it to this moment—and that you chose to pull these devotions off the shelf and into your hands. Every word on these pages was written with a receptive heart toward YHWH, with prayers that they would also meet you right where you are, whispering to your soul and reminding you that you are never, ever alone.

My hope is that something here has touched a place in you that truly matters. I pray you'll find healing stirring within your own heart and begin to see your story through the tender eyes of our loving Father. May you welcome transformation, self-discovery, new beginnings, and a deeper closeness with God—Yahweh, He knows you by name.

The same Yahweh who carried me through seasons of deep sorrow can carry you too—again and again, as many times as you need. You are chosen. You are seen. You are loved by a God who still speaks, still heals, and never lets go. It doesn't matter how broken or unjust your past may feel, how heavy the blame you've carried, or how uncertain the road ahead seems. He knows you. He cares. He always knows what's best.

May these devotions be a lifeline when the waters feel high, a gentle light when the path seems dark, and a steady anchor when everything around you shifts. Even in the quiet, God is with you.

So keep seeking. Keep loving and praying. Keep healing, dreaming, and daring to live fully.

Remember, we grieve because we hurt, and hurt comes from loving deeply and purely.

Keep rising—because with Him, you always can.

Please enjoy the reflective and supportive pages that I've created for you below.

Shalom, love and blessings,

ANDREYAH

MORE ABOUT THE AUTHOR

AndreYAH Maria Hernandez Black
(Also known as Queen AndreYAH)

AndreYAH Maria Hernandez Black is a visionary, licensed evangelist, alternative medicine practitioner, performing artist, documentary filmmaker, and author whose life bridges spirituality and the transformative power of music and art. Rooted in holistic health since 1985 and global ministry since 2004, she uplifts communities through arts education, wellness, entrepreneurship, and outreach.

A recipient of many prestigious honors—including the **Belle Zeller Award, Global**

Citizenship Alliance Seminar Fellowship, and Thomas W. Smith Award, amongst others—AndreYAH's global work has taken her across the United States, Africa, South America, Germany, Canada, Austria, and Russia, where she has served as a minister, an arts educator, choreographer and performing artist both on stage and in media. Through her gifts, she is a messenger of hope, empowerment, and sustainable transformation.

Her debut book, **Revelations for Resilience: Whispers from the Divine**, is an inspirational poetic devotional designed to awaken inner strength and **deepen connection to the Divine through life's most challenging moments**—guiding readers who have endured hardship or face trials toward healing, hope, and resilience.

Through her poetry, music, films, and artistry, AndreYAH continues to inspire others to live with faith, purpose, and reverence for the sacred dimensions of life.

www.ingramcontent.com/pod-product-compliance
Lightning Source LLC
Chambersburg PA
CBHW040726060526
44119CB00084B/342